Animal Pranksters

Foureye Butterflyfish

by Julie Murray

T0020295

2

Dash!
LEVELED READERS
An Imprint of Abdo Zoom • abdobooks.com

2 Dash!
LEVELED READERS

Level 1 – Beginning
Short and simple sentences with familiar words or patterns for children who are beginning to understand how letters and sounds go together.

Level 2 – Emerging
Longer words and sentences with more complex language patterns for readers who are practicing common words and letter sounds.

Level 3 – Transitional
More developed language and vocabulary for readers who are becoming more independent.

THIS BOOK CONTAINS RECYCLED MATERIALS

abdobooks.com

Published by Abdo Zoom, a division of ABDO, PO Box 398166, Minneapolis, Minnesota 55439. Copyright © 2023 by Abdo Consulting Group, Inc. International copyrights reserved in all countries. No part of this book may be reproduced in any form without written permission from the publisher. Dash!™ is a trademark and logo of Abdo Zoom.

Printed in the United States of America, North Mankato, Minnesota.
052022
092022

Photo Credits: Alamy, Getty Images, Minden Pictures, Shutterstock
Production Contributors: Kenny Abdo, Jennie Forsberg, Grace Hansen, John Hansen
Design Contributors: Candice Keimig, Neil Klinepier

Library of Congress Control Number: 2021950309

Publisher's Cataloging in Publication Data

Names: Murray, Julie, author.
Title: Foureye butterflyfish / by Julie Murray.
Description: Minneapolis, Minnesota : Abdo Zoom, 2023 | Series: Animal pranksters | Includes online resources and index.
Identifiers: ISBN 9781098228347 (lib. bdg.) | ISBN 9781644947616 (pbk.) | ISBN 9781098229184 (ebook) | ISBN 9781098229603 (Read-to-Me ebook)
Subjects: LCSH: Butterflyfish--Juvenile literature. | Coral reef fishes--Juvenile literature. | Marine fishes--Behavior--Juvenile literature. | Zoology--Juvenile literature.
Classification: DDC 597.03--dc23

Table of Contents

Foureye
Butterflyfish

Foureye butterflyfish live along the eastern coast of North and South America. They are also found in the Gulf of Mexico and the Caribbean Sea.

They live in shallow water where there are lots of fish eggs, worms, and **crustaceans** to eat.

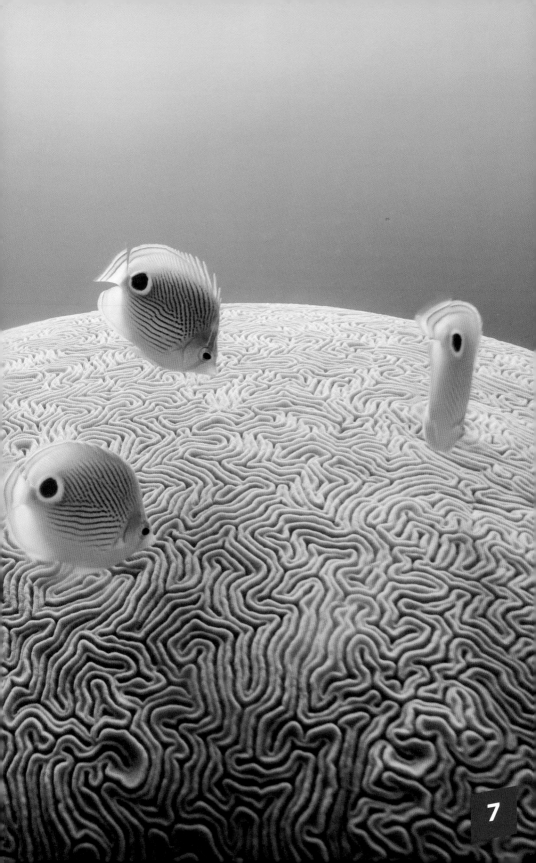

They have flat, disk-shaped bodies. They can easily swim around **coral reefs** and sea grass.

They are small fish.
They are around just
four inches (10 cm) long.

Their bodies are light gray with dark stripes. Their bellies and fins are yellow.

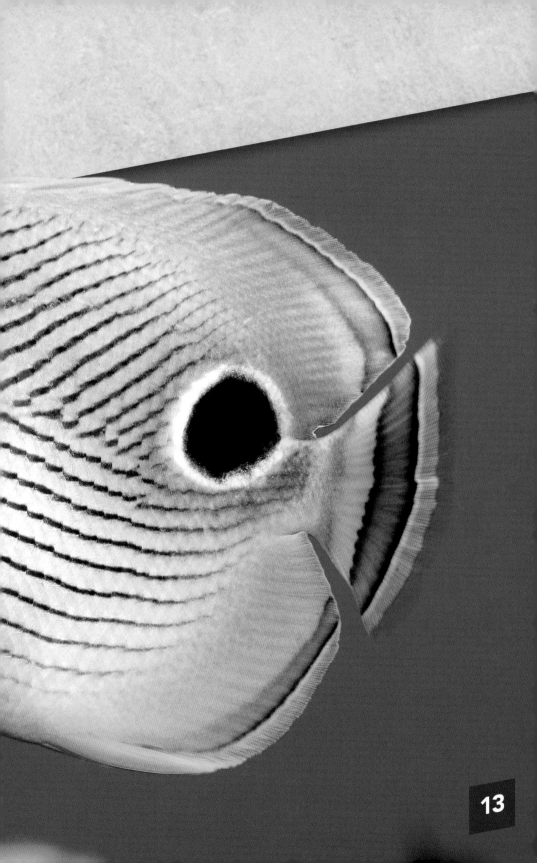

13

The fish has two large black spots near its tail fin. These are fake eyes! The fish's real eyes are covered by dark stripes.

Fake Eyes

Predators are tricked by the fish's fake eyes. They can't tell which end is the head.

This "prank" creates **confusion**. It gives the fish a chance to get away.

It looks like the fish is swimming backwards when it flees!

More Facts

- Foureye butterflyfish are one of few fish that stay together for life. They are often seen in pairs.

- They are very **agile**. They can even swim upside down!

- Because they are small and beautiful, they are popular aquarium fish.

Glossary

agile – able to move quickly and gracefully.

confusion – the state of being confused.

coral reef – an underwater structure that rises up from the bottom of the sea and is made up of the hard skeletons of tiny sea animals called corals.

crustacean – an animal, including crabs, lobsters, and shrimps, with a hard, jointed shell that lives in fresh or salt water.

predator – an animal that eats other animals for food.

Index

Online Resources

Booklinks
NONFICTION NETWORK
FREE! ONLINE NONFICTION RESOURCES

To learn more about foureye butterflyfish, please visit **abdobooklinks.com** or scan this QR code. These links are routinely monitored and updated to provide the most current information available.